Little Pebble™

Our Families

T0085130

Grandfathers Are Part of a Family

by Lucia Raatma

CAPSTONE PRESS
a capstone imprint

Little Pebble is published by Capstone Press,
1710 Roe Crest Drive, North Mankato, Minnesota 56003
www.mycapstone.com

Copyright © 2018 by Capstone Press, a Capstone imprint. All rights reserved.
No part of this publication may be reproduced in whole or in part, or stored in a retrieval system, or transmitted in any form or by any means, electronic, mechanical, photocopying, recording, or otherwise, without written permission of the publisher.

Library of Congress Cataloging-in-Publication Data is available on the Library of Congress website

ISBN: 978-1-5157-7458-7 (library binding)
ISBN: 978-1-5157-7469-3 (paperback)
written by Lucia Raatma

Editorial Credits
Christianne Jones, editor; Juliette Peters, designer;
Wanda Winch, media researcher; Laura Manthe, production specialist

Photo Credits
Capstone Studio: Karon Dubke, 5, 7, 13, 15, 19, 21; Shutterstock: Angelina Babii, paper texture, Burlingham, 9, Diego Cervo, 1, Dragon Images, cover, Monkey Business Images, 11, Teguh Mujiono, tree design; Thinkstock: Photodisc, 17

Printed in the United States 5390

Table of Contents

Grandfathers 4

What Grandfathers Do 8

Glossary 22

Read More 23

Internet Sites 23

Index 24

Grandfathers

A grandfather is the father of your mother or father. He can be called grandpa.

A grandpa may have grandsons. He may also have granddaughters.

What Grandfathers Do

Wilson's grandpa goes to work. He is a teacher.

Jack's grandpa lives near Jack. They like to fish.

Jacy's grandpa is a farmer.

He works hard.

TRAC

Jada lives with her grandpa.
They like to play and laugh.

Brad's grandpa lives far away. They talk on the phone.

Teddy likes to ride his bike. His grandpa helps him.

VIGOR

Grandpas help.

They love.

They hug.

Glossary

granddaughter—a female child of one's son or daughter

grandfather—the father of a mother or father

grandson—a male child of one's son or daughter

Read More

Ajmera, Maya. *Our Grandparents: A Global Album.* Watertown, MA: Charlesbridge, 2010.

Harris, Robie H. *Who's in My Family?* All About Our Families. Somerville, MA: Candlewick, 2012.

Hunter, Nick. *Finding Out About Your Family History.* Mankato, MN: Heinemann-Raintree, 2015.

Internet Sites

FactHound offers a safe, fun way to find Internet sites related to this book. All of the sites on FactHound have been researched by our staff.

Here's all you do:
Visit *www.facthound.com*
Type in this code: 9781515774587

Index

biking, 18

farmers, 12

fathers, 4

fishing, 10

granddaughters, 6

grandsons, 6

helping, 18, 20

hugging, 20

laughing, 14

loving, 20

mothers, 4

playing, 14

talking on the phone, 16

working, 8, 12